T0025681

LAUGH
-Out-
LOUD

ADVENTURE

JOKES
for KIDS

LAUGH
-Out-
LOUD
ADVENTURE

JOKES
for KIDS

ROB ELLIOTT

HARPER
An Imprint of HarperCollins Publishers

Library of Congress Control Number 2019941420

ISBN 978-0-06-274870-6

21 22 23   PC/BRR   10 9 8 7 6 5 4 3

❖

First Edition

To the international students who have shared their lives with me these past few years: Rita, David M, Icey, Jonita, Hayeong, Stefanie, Lucero, Kairu, David, and Michael. Knowing you is the best kind of adventure!

- -

Q: Why were there lizards all over the bathroom wall?

A: Because it had been rep-tiled.

Q: How do you call an alligator?

A: You croco-dial your phone.

Knock, knock.

Who's there?

Wildebeest.

Wildebeest who?

Wildebeest marry Belle at the end of the story?

Knock, knock.

Who's there?

Parmesan.

Parmesan who?

Do I have your parmesan to come in?

Q: What do you call a squid with only six arms?

A: A hexa-pus.

Q: How does the runner like her eggs?

A: With a dash of pepper.

Knock, knock.

Who's there?

Wanda.

Wanda who?

Wanda go hiking with me?

Q: Why did the clock go to jail?

A: For killing time!

Q: Why did the butcher work so hard?

A: He had to bring home the bacon.

Q: Why did the polar bear spit out the clown?

A: He tasted funny.

Knock, knock.

Who's there?

Joanna.

Joanna who?

Joanna go to the races today?

Q: Why did the sea captain throw peanut butter in the ocean?

A: He wanted to attract the jellyfish.

Q: What do you get when you cross an astronaut and a sea creature?

A: A starfish.

Q: What's a sailor's least favorite vegetable?

A: A leek.

Knock, knock.

Who's there?

Llama.

Llama who?

Llama in! It's cold out here!

Knock, knock.

Who's there?

Wooden shoe.

Wooden shoe who?

Wooden shoe like to go canoeing today?

Q: **What kind of vegetables wear socks?**

A: Potatoes.

Q: **Why don't fish ever go on vacation?**

A: Because they're always in schools.

Q: **What kind of snake leads the band?**

A: A boa conductor.

Q: **What is a grasshopper's favorite sport?**

A: Cricket.

Q: Why do babies like basketball?

A: They're always dribbling.

Parent: How was school today?

Child: There was a kidnapping in our class today.

Parent: Oh, no! What happened?

Child: The teacher woke him up and gave him detention.

Q: What kind of grades did the ship captain get?

A: High Cs.

Q: How do you throw a party on Mars?

A: You planet.

Knock, knock.

Who's there?

Wool.

Wool who?

Wool you go on an adventure with me?

Knock, knock.

Who's there?

Philip.

Philip who?

Philip the car and we can be on our way.

Q: What do boxers do when they're thirsty?

A: They get some punch.

Knock, knock.

Who's there?

Joe King.

Joe King who?

Oh, no one. I'm just joking.

Q: What did the man do when he was standing out in a thunderstorm?

A: He hailed a cab.

Q: **What is an ape's favorite kind of cookie?**

A: Chocolate chimp.

Q: **Where do you park your rocket on Mars?**

A: At a parking meteor.

Q: **What did the horse do after the trail ride?**

A: It hit the hay.

Q: **Why did the kids always fight during math class?**

A: There was division among them.

Q: What do bakers and cats have in common?

A: They both like to start from scratch.

Q: What do you get if you put a pig on a racetrack?

A: A road hog!

Q: What did the computer programmer do at lunchtime?

A: She had a byte.

Q: Why are night crawlers so smart?

A: They're bookworms.

Q: Why did the clock get in trouble?

A: It wouldn't stop tocking.

Q: Where do tarantulas get their information?

A: From the World Wide Web.

Q: Why did the toilet go to the doctor?

A: It looked flushed!

Q: Why did the karate instructor wear earplugs?

A: He had sensei-tive ears.

Q: What did the leopard say after dinner?

A: That hit the spot.

Q: How do you get a baby astronaut to stop crying?

A: You rocket!

Q: How does an elephant get ready for vacation?

A: It packs its trunk.

Q: **Why did the maple tree watch romantic movies?**

A: It was sappy.

Q: **Who is the best dancer at the monsters' ball?**

A: The boogieman.

Q: **Why did the snickerdoodle refuse to be eaten?**

A: It was one tough cookie.

Q: **Why did the pony get in trouble?**

A: It was horsing around.

Knock, knock.

Who's there?

Iguana.

Iguana who?

Iguana go mountain climbing with you!

Q: What is a black belt's favorite drink?

A: Kara-tea.

Knock, knock.

Who's there?

Russian.

Russian who?

I'm Russian around to get ready!

Q: What did the atom do when it was ready to go?

A: It split.

Q: What kind of shoes do ninjas wear?

A: Sneakers.

Q: Why did the man quit being a dentist?

A: He didn't have the patients for it.

Q: Why did the chicken travel the world?

A: It was tired of being cooped up!

Q: When do ducks get out of bed?

A: At the quack of dawn.

Q: Why couldn't the librarian ever go on vacation?

A: She was always booked.

Q: How did the monkey escape from the zoo?

A: In a hot-air baboon.

Q: Why did the robot go on a camping trip?

A: To recharge its batteries.

Q: Why was it so windy in the football stadium?

A: There were thousands of fans!

Q: Why did the pelican run out of money?

A: It had a big bill.

Q: Why was the valley laughing?

A: Because the mountains were hill-arious!

Knock, knock.

Who's there?

Funnel.

Funnel who?

The funnel start once we head to the beach.

Q: Why did the student do his home-work in a helicopter?

A: He wanted a higher education.

Q: How do you make a strawberry shake?

A: Tell it a scary story.

Q: **What did the horse say to the cowboy when it ran out of hay?**

A: That's the last straw!

Q: **What do you get when a butcher and a baker get married?**

A: Meat loaf.

Knock, knock.

Who's there?

Radio.

Radio who?

Radio not, here we come!

Q: What is the easiest kind of lid to open?

A: Your eyelid.

Q: How do mountains stay warm in the winter?

A: With their snowcaps.

Q: Why did the boy bring his computer to the beach?

A: He wanted to surf the internet.

Q: How did the polar bear get to work?

A: On a motor-icicle.

Q: Why did the duck go skydiving?

A: It wasn't chicken!

Knock, knock.

Who's there?

Europe.

Europe who?

Europe very early this morning.

Q: When are all the books in the library the same color?

A: When they're read.

Q: What do you get when you cross a bicycle and a flower?

A: A bike petal.

Q: What did the sailor say every morning?

A: "Seas the day!"

Q: What is a whale's favorite vegetable?

A: A sea cucumber.

Q: What do you get when your dad rides a bike?

A: A pop-cycle.

Q: Why do surgeons make great comedians?

A: Because they always have you in stitches.

Q: What do you call a dancing sheep?

A: A baaa-llerina.

Q: Where did the skiers fall in love?

A: At the snowball.

Q: Why did the cow become an acrobat?

A: It was so flexi-bull!

Q: How does Santa find his way home?

A: He uses his snow globe.

Q: How do you catch a school of fish?

A: With a bookworm.

Q: What do grizzlies do when they meet a clown?

A: They just grin and bear it!

Andy: Did you hear about the panther that told the boy he wouldn't eat him?

Daniel: No, what happened?

Andy: He was lion.

Q: Where do tropical fish keep their work?

A: In a reef-case.

Q: What happened when Frankenstein heard the joke?

A: He was in stitches!

Q: What do bananas and acrobats have in common?

A: They can both do splits.

Q: Where can you learn how to make a banana split?

A: Sundae school.

Q: What do you call it when two boa constrictors fall in love?

A: A crush.

Knock, knock.

Who's there?

Wood.

Wood who?

Wood you like to go swimming with

me?

Q: Why did the dog get kicked out of

the soccer game?

A: He was playing too ruff!

Knock, knock.

Who's there?

Justin.

Justin who?

Justin time to go snowboarding!

Knock, knock.

Who's there?

Noah.

Noah who?

Noah great place to go camping?

Q: Why did the hungry lion eat the dentist?

A: He looked so filling.

Knock, knock.

Who's there?

Howard.

Howard who?

Howard you like to go on a safari?

Q: Why can't you give your dog the TV remote?

A: It'll keep hitting the paws button.

Q: Why did the snail take a nap?

A: It was feeling sluggish.

Q: What do you call a sleepy wood-cutter?

A: A slumber-jack.

Q: Why was the climbing rope anx-ious?

A: It was getting all strung out!

Q: How did Mary feel when her little lamb followed her to school?

A: Sheepish!

Q: Why was the scuba diver embarrassed?

A: He saw the ocean's bottom.

Q: Why wouldn't the chicken grow?

A: It had smallpox.

Knock, knock.

Who's there?

Peter.

Peter who?

Peter boots on so we can go hiking!

Q: What do you give a farmer who sings out of tune?

A: A pitchfork.

Knock, knock.

Who's there?

Muffin.

Muffin who?

Muffin to do today—let's go have some fun!

Q: What's a robot's favorite snack?

A: Computer chips.

Q: Why do snowmen melt if you take their carrots away?

A: It makes them boiling mad!

Knock, knock.

Who's there?

Luke.

Luke who?

Luke over there—a bear is coming!

Q: What do you get when a T. rex and a brontosaurus play football?

A: Dino-scores.

Luke: I'm so tired of climbing this big hill!

Zack: Oh, get over it!

Q: Why did the whales watch the sunset?

A: They wanted a sea-nic view.

Q: Why did the baker become an actor?

A: He wanted to play a roll.

Q: Why did the vampire join the circus?

A: He wanted to be an acro-bat.

Q: What is the biggest bug in the world?

A: The mam-moth.

Q: Why did the coffee file a police report?

A: It was mugged.

Knock, knock.

Who's there?

Dishes.

Dishes who?

Dishes the police. Come out with your hands up!

Q: **What do you get when you cross a knife and your front lawn?**

A: Blades of grass!

Knock, knock.

Who's there?

Norway.

Norway who?

Norway am I parachute jumping out of a plane!

Q: **How does a polar bear build its house?**

A: Igloos it together.

Q: Where does Mickey Mouse keep his groceries?

A: In a Minnie fridge.

Q: What happened when the turkey and the rooster got in a fight?

A: The turkey got the stuffing knocked out of him.

Tom: Hey, want to hear another insect joke?

Jim: No, stop bugging me!

Q: Why did the lumberjack get fired?

A: He axed too many questions.

Q: What do conductors and mountain climbers have in common?

A: They both like the terrain.

Q: What do ghosts wear to climb a mountain?

A: Hiking boo-ts!

Q: What do you get when you cross a dog and a cow?

A: Hound beef.

Q: What is the most famous kind of drink?

A: A celebri-tea!

Q: How did the fisherman finish in half the time?

A: He was e-fish-ent!

Q: Why do skeletons always laugh at your jokes?

A: They find everything humerus.

Q: How do you light things in a stadium?

A: With a soccer match.

Q: **How do snowmen stay warm at night?**

A: With a blanket of snow.

Q: **How did the fisherman have his tonsils taken out?**

A: He went to a sturgeon.

Q: **What do you get if you put coffee on your head?**

A: A cap-puccino.

Q: **Why did the man put his car in the oven?**

A: He wanted to drive a hot rod.

Q: How did the pepper catch a cold?

A: It was a little chili.

Q: How did the boulder go to bed?

A: He rocked himself to sleep.

Q: What do you get if you cross a pillow and a can of soda?

A: A soft drink!

Q: What is the difference between a dog and a flea?

A: A dog can flea but a flea can't dog.

Q: Why was the dog laughing?

A: Someone gave it a funny bone.

Knock, knock.

Who's there?

Defeat.

Defeat who?

Defeat are really sore after a long hike!

Knock, knock.

Who's there?

Anita.

Anita who?

Anita get out of the house for some fresh air!

Q: What do baseball teams and bakers have in common?

A: They both need good batters.

Q: What's something you serve but can never eat?

A: A tennis ball.

- -

Q: What did the shark do when it caught a cold?

A: It took some vitamin sea.

Knock, knock.

Who's there?

Wendy.

Wendy who?

Wendy we go to the skate park?

Knock, knock.

Who's there?

Pecan.

Pecan who?

Pecan someone your own size!

Q: What happened when the sea lions fell in love?

A: They sealed it with a kiss.

Q: What do bats do in their free time?

A: They just hang out!

Q: Why did the librarian become a detective?

A: She wanted to go undercover.

Q: Why shouldn't you tell jokes to an egg?

A: You don't want it to crack up!

Q: What happened when the dalmatian took a bath?

A: It became spotless.

Q: Why do frogs love baseball?

A: They like to catch the fly balls.

Q: Why did the baby become a scientist?

A: She liked her formulas.

Q: Where do swimmers go for fun?

A: To the dive-in movies.

Q: What do you call it when quarters rain from the sky?

A: Climate change!

Q: What's a grasshopper's favorite sport?

A: Cricket.

Knock, knock.

Who's there?

Alpaca.

Alpaca who?

Alpaca lunch for our hike today.

Q: What do you get when you cross a chicken and a dog?

A: A clucker spaniel.

Q: Why do boxers make bad comedi-ans?

A: They always start with the punch line.

Q: Why did the man's jacket catch on fire?

A: It was a blazer.

Knock, knock.

Who's there?

Hugo.

Hugo who?

Hugo first and I'll follow!

Q: Why did the cowboy take his horse to the vet?

A: It had hay fever.

Q: What kind of shoes do butchers wear?

A: Meat loafers.

Q: What do race car drivers eat before they race?

A: Car-bohydrates.

Q: What gets harder to catch the faster you run?

A: Your breath.

Q: Why can't you win a race against a barber?

A: He knows all the shortcuts.

Q: What happened when the skunk wrote a book?

A: It became a best smeller!

Q: What do you get when you cross a turtle and a porcupine?

A: A slowpoke!

Knock, knock.

Who's there?

Donut.

Donut who?

Donut you want to come outside today?

Q: What happened to the boy who swallowed his trombone?

A: He tooted his own horn!

Q: What kind of fish likes bubble gum?

A: A blowfish.

Q: Why wouldn't the sheep stop talking?

A: It liked to ram-ble!

Q: Why did the spider steal the sports car?

A: He wanted to take it for a spin.

- - - - - - - - - - - - - - - - - - -

Q: Why did the sun move away from the moon?

A: It wanted some space.

Q: How come it didn't cost anything to go bungee jumping?

A: It was a free fall!

Q: What kind of clothes do dogs wear in the summer?

Λ: Pants.

Q: Where do scarecrows go for fun?

A: On field trips.

- - - - - - - - - - - - - - - - - - -

Q: Why are mountains always tired?

A: Because they don't Everest!

Knock, knock.

Who's there?

Sara.

Sara who?

Sara nother way around this lake?

Q: Why is tennis such a noisy sport?

A: The players raise a lot of racket.

Q: Why can't you play hide-and-seek

with mountains?

A: They're always peak-ing.

Knock, knock.

Who's there?

Taco.

Taco who?

Taco 'bout what you want to do today.

Q: What do you get when you cross an alien and a tea party?

A: Flying saucers.

Q: What do you get when you cross a pig and a toolbox?

A: A ham-mer.

Q: What do you call a banana store?

A: A monkey business!

Q: **What do you get when you put an opera singer in the bathtub?**

A: A soap-rano!

Q: **Why did the chemistry teacher stop telling jokes?**

A: He could never get a reaction.

Q: **What are a horse's favorite snacks?**

A: Straw-berries and hay-zelnuts.

Q: **What do you call a boomerang that doesn't come back?**

A: A stick.

Q: How does a bug get around in the winter?

A: In a snowmo-beetle.

Q: How does a skater cut up her steak?

A: With Roller-blades!

Q: How do athletes stay cool in the summer?

A: They stay close to their fans.

Q: Why did the guitar player go to the auto mechanic?

A: She needed a tune-up.

Rita: Do you know where they cooked the first French fries?

Stephanie: France?

Rita: No, in Greece!

Q: Why did they kick the pig off the basketball court?

A: It was hogging the ball!

Sam: Why did the alien grow a garden in space?

Marcus: It had a green thumb!

Knock, knock.

Who's there?

Riley.

Riley who?

I Riley think you should wear a helmet if you skateboard!

Q: Why was the whale always painting?

A: It was art-sea.

Q: What does an astronaut do with a bar of soap?

A: She takes a meteor shower!

Q: How does a lobster like its eggs?

A: With a pinch of salt.

Knock, knock.

   Who's there?

Toad.

   Toad who?

I toad my mom we'd be back in time

   for dinner.

Knock, knock.

   Who's there?

Avenue.

   Avenue who?

Avenue seen the Grand Canyon

   before?

Susie: Want to go see the llamas?

Sofia: That sounds fun!

Susie: Alpaca suitcase.

Knock, knock.

Who's there?

Parker.

Parker who?

I parker bike in my garage.

Knock, knock.

Who's there?

Iguana.

Iguana who?

Iguana ride my scooter to the park today.

Knock, knock.

Who's there?

Harry.

Harry who?

Harry up so we can get going!

Knock, knock.

Who's there?

Finley.

Finley who?

Finley it's Saturday—let's go have some fun!

Knock, knock.

Who's there?

Toby.

Toby who?

Toby safe, wear a life jacket when you're sailing.

Knock, knock.

Who's there?

Heidi.

Heidi who?

Heidi picnic basket so the bears don't get it!

Knock, knock.

Who's there?

Sawyer.

Sawyer who?

I sawyer sister at the park today!

Jim: I want to canoe down the river today.

Sue: You otter do that!

Q: Why did the whale need a hug?

A: It was blue.

Q: Why did the driver squeeze his car?

A: Because it was a lemon.

Q: What do sharks eat for breakfast?

A: Muf-fins.

Q: Why did the baker make so much bread?

A: Because it was kneaded.

Q: What do you get when you put glue on your doughnut?

A: A paste-ry.

Q: How many skunks does it take to change a lightbulb?

A: Just a phew.

Q: What makes a pirate angry?

A: When you take away the P.

Hannah: There's an octopus in my bathtub!

Olivia: You're just squid-ing me.

Q: Why didn't the hunter eat sandwiches anymore?

A: He quit cold turkey.

Q: How did the scientist freshen up his lab?

A: He used experi-mints.

Q: What's an astronaut's favorite kind of cookie?

A: Rocket chip.

Knock, knock.

Who's there?

Irish.

Irish who?

Irish we would go on more adventures!

Tim: Hey, Mark. You want to hear my underwear joke?

Mark: Is it clean?

Q: **What word has three letters and starts with gas?**

A: A car.

Q: **Why did the girl join the soccer team?**

A: She thought she'd get a kick out of it.

Q: **What's a guitar player's favorite sport?**

A: Bass-jumping

Q: **Where do you put fish once you catch them?**

A: In a cof-fin.

**Q: Why did the student run around
the school before a test?**

A: To jog her memory.

Q: Why don't crocodiles ever get lost?

A: They're great navi-gators.

Q: Why are story writers always cold?

A: They always have drafts on their
desks.

Q: What kind of vegetable do hippos like?

A: Zoo-cchini.

Q: What kind of fruits do boxers eat?

A: Black-and-blue berries.

Q: What do you call a ram that tells a lot of jokes?

A: A silly goat.

Q: How did the conductor get to work?

A: On the bandwagon.

Q: What did the sharks say at the all-you-can-eat buffet?

A: Let's dive in!

Q: What do you get when you cross a pilot and a swimming pool?

A: A skydiver!

Q: Why did the fisher run out of money?

A: He couldn't keep his business afloat.

Knock, knock.

Who's there?

Rugby.

Rugby who?

My rugby needing some vacuuming today!

Q: Why wouldn't the bike wake up?

A: It was two tired.

Q: What do you get when you cross a pig and a tree?

A: A porcupine.

Q: What kind of bug is hard to catch?

A: A Fris-bee.

Q: How did the koala build its house?

A: With its bear hands.

Knock, knock.

Who's there?

Canopy.

Canopy who?

Canopy outside when we go camping?

Q: What do a judge and a tennis player have in common?

A: They both go to court every day.

Q: How many golfers does it take to change a lightbulb?

A: Fore!

Q: **What do you get when you cross an ox and a canoe?**

A: A ka-yak.

Q: **What do you call it when two black belts fall in love?**

A: Martial hearts.

Q: **Why did the secret agent get fired?**

A: He was clue-less.

Q: **What happened when the tigers escaped from the zoo?**

A: It became a cat-astrophe!

Q: What is a skunk's favorite color?

A: Pew-ter.

Q: Why did the detective fall asleep at his desk?

A: He had a pillow-case.

Q: What do eagles eat for lunch?

A: Fish and chirps.

Q: Where do you keep your pillow when you're camping?

A: In a knapsack.

What do you call a mountain climber?

Cliff.

What do you call a fisherman?

Rod.

What do you call a barber?

Harry.

What do you call a housekeeper?

Dustin.

What do you call a cat burglar?

Rob.

- -

What do you call a librarian?

Paige.

What do you call a basketball player?

Duncan.

What do you call a weight lifter?

Jim.

What do you call a painter?

Art.

What do you call an archaeologist?

Doug.

Q: Why did the cowboy go crazy?

A: He was de-ranged.

Knock, knock.

Who's there?

Firewood.

Firewood who?

Firewood keep us warm when we're camping.

Q: What do you get if you put bananas in your tent?

A: Slipping bags!

Q: Why did the girl take a blender on a hike?

A: So she could make trail mix.

Q: What kind of bird builds skyscrapers?

A: The crane.

Knock, knock.

Who's there?

Mustache.

Mustache who?

I mustache you if we can go rock climbing today!

Q: How much did it cost to build the beaver dam?

A: An arm and a log.

Q: Why didn't the fisherman get his email?

A: He was out of net-work.

Q: Why do baseball umpires always get dessert?

A: They're good at cleaning their plates.

Q: What do you get when you cross a washing machine and a bike?

A: A spin cycle!

Q: Why did the dentist coach the basketball team?

A: He knew the drills.

Q: To what type of fish should you never tell a secret?

A: A largemouth bass!

Q: What do you do with a worn-out baseball?

A: You pitch it.

Q: Why do farmers like to jump rope?

A: They never skip a beet!

Amy: What kind of nut do you like in your trail mix?

Susy: Cashew.

Amy: Bless you!

Q: What do you get if you throw a microphone in the ocean?

A: A starfish.

Knock, knock.

Who's there?

Annie.

Annie who?

Annie-body else up for a little skydiving today?

Knock, knock.

Who's there?

Tickle.

Tickle who?

A tickle make your dog start itching.

Knock, knock.

Who's there?

Melon.

Melon who?

You're one in a melon!

Q: Why do dragons sleep during the day?

A: They like to fight knights.

Q: How did the snail feel after running a 5K?

A: Sluggish.

Knock, knock.

Who's there?

Feline.

Feline who?

Feline like it's time for an adventure!

Q: What happens when you cross a cow and a comedian?

A: It's udderly ridiculous!

Knock, knock.

Who's there?

Mabel.

Mabel who?

Mabel isn't working, so you'll have to keep knocking.

Q: Why can't chickens play baseball?

A: They hit only fowl balls.

Q: What kind of bird rides in a limo?

A: An ost-rich.

Knock, knock.

Who's there?

Lucas.

Lucas who?

Lucas time to play outside!

Knock, knock.

Who's there?

Raymond.

Raymond who?

Raymond me to wear my helmet when I'm biking.

Q: Why did the math teacher go berry picking?

A: He really liked Pi.

**Q: How do you unlock the racing
stables?**

A: With a joc-key.

**Q: What do you get when you cross a
fish and a radio?**

A: A catchy tuna!

Knock, knock.

Who's there?

Waffle.

Waffle who?

**Sorry, the waffle weather made me
late!**

Laura: My pickles won a blue ribbon at the fair!

Mary: That's a very big dill!

Q: Why did the spider get a job at the computer company?

A: He was a great web designer.

Q: What is a cat's favorite sport?

A: Meow-tain climbing.

Knock, knock.

Who's there?

Douglas.

Douglas who?

Douglas is full of water if you're thirsty.

Knock, knock.

Who's there?

Money.

Money who?

Money is sore from running all day.

Knock, knock.

Who's there?

Alaska.

Alaska who?

Alaska one more time if you can come out and play!

Q: What do fish like best at the playground?

A: The sea-saw.

Q: Why did the dairy farmer cross the road?

A: To get to the udder side.

Knock, knock.

Who's there?

Milton.

Milton who?

Milton snow means no more sledding.

Knock, knock.

Who's there?

Welcome.

Welcome who?

Welcome with you when you go for a ride.

Q: Where do the manatees keep all their money?

A: In the river-bank!

Joe: Why did you put a kazoo in your lunchbox?

Jim: I wanted a hum sandwich!

Q: What kind of mountain can talk?

A: Pikes Speak!

Q: Why did the duck get sent to the principal's office?

A: It was a wise-quacker.

Q: What do a bank and a football game have in common?

A: They both have quarters.

Paul: Do you want to try fencing with me?

Pete: I'll take a stab at it.

Knock, knock.

Who's there?

Canoe.

Canoe who?

Canoe tell me where the paddles are?

Q: Why are turtles always throwing parties?

A: They like to shell-ebrate!

Q: What did the horse do when she fell in love?

A: She got mare-ried.

Q: What do you get if you cross a snail and a camera?

A: Shell-fies.

Q: Why did the rabbit ride the roller coaster?

A: It was looking for a hare-raising experience!

Knock, knock.

Who's there?

Odyssey.

Odyssey who?

Odyssey who's at the door before I answer it.

Q: What do rhinos and credit cards have in common?

A: They both like to charge!

Knock, knock.

Who's there?

Wander.

Wander who?

Wander if we'll go to the ocean this summer.

Q: What do you call a lady who lost all her money?

A: Miss Fortune.

Q: Why couldn't the man get reservations at the restaurant on the moon?

A: It was full.

Q: What did the skunk say after it sprayed the campers?

A: You're so scent-sitive!

Q: Why did the tree go to the beauty shop?

A: It needed to have its roots done.

Q: Why did the boy wear a lampshade for a hat?

A: He felt light-headed.

Q: Where do you find flying rabbits?

A: The hare force.

Q: **What do you call a monster that can really focus?**

A: An aware-wolf.

Q: **When is a plumber like a scuba diver?**

A: When he takes the plunge!

Q: **Why did the fisherman go to the doctor?**

A: He was having trouble with his herring!

Q: **What is a giraffe's favorite fruit?**

A: Neck-tarines!

Knock, knock.

Who's there?

Pasture.

Pasture who?

Pasture house on the way to the park and thought I'd stop by.

Q: What did the chef say after he cooked the steak?

A: Well done!

James: Did you hear the joke about the hot-air balloon?

Jack: It went right over my head!

Knock, knock.

Who's there?

Weasel.

Weasel who?

Weasel be late if you don't open the door!

Q: What do you call a sad dog?

A: A melan-collie.

Q: Why shouldn't you play with a skunk?

A: It's just common scents.

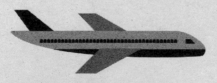

Q: What kind of fruit turns to stone?

A: A pome-granite.

Q: Why don't bakeries let their employees shave?

A: Because they need their whisk-ers.

Q: Where do you buy medicine for your chickens?

A: At the farm-acy.

Q: What did the astronaut take for his headache?

A: A space capsule.

Q: **Why did the train go to the play-ground?**

A: To blow off some steam.

Q: **How do you stay happy when you're running a marathon?**

A: One s-mile at a time!

Q: **What do you do if you catch too many fish?**

A: You scale back!

Q: **What do baseball players eat for dessert?**

A: Bunt (Bundt) cake!

Q: Why won't lobsters laugh at my jokes?

A: Because they're crabby!

Q: What do motorcycle racers eat for lunch?

A: Fast food.

Q: Why did the basketball player throw his banana in the hoop?

A: He wanted to make a fruit basket.

Q: Why do cows go to the gym?

A: To work their calves.

Q: What do night crawlers do before they go for a run?

A: Worm-ups.

Q: What does a basketball player do before she blows out her birthday candles?

A: She makes a swish!

Q: How do you know if you're on a lazy volcano?

A: It's not very active.

Q: What happened when the boy got toilet paper for his birthday?

A: He had a pity potty!

Q: Why did the king go to the dentist?

A: He needed his crown fixed.

Q: What did the mountain say to the valley?

A: You're gorges!

Q: How do you know which flag is the best?

A: You take a pole.

Q: **Why did the man dial the canary on the phone?**

A: He wanted to try a birdcall.

Q: **What does a baker do for fun?**

A: Bun-gee jumping!

Q: **What happened to the singer after he was hit by lightning?**

A: He became a shock star.

Q: **Why can't you tell a whale anything?**

A: It can't keep a sea-cret.

Q: Why didn't the eagle practice flying?

A: She thought she could just wing it!

Q: How do you get your mom to buy you a kitten?

A: With a little purr-suasion.

Q: What do you call someone with an underwater race car?

A: A scuba driver!

Q: How does it feel if a grizzly steps on your toe?

A: Unbearable!

Tailor: Do you like your new suit?

Customer: It's sew-sew.

Knock, knock.

Who's there?

Candy.

Candy who?

Candy kids come out and play?

Q: Why is bowling like a flat tire?

A: You want a spare.

Q: Why did the spy come out at bed-time?

A: He only works undercovers.

Q: Why don't frogs tell the truth?

A: They're am-fib-ians.

Q: What's a cow's favorite game in gym class?

A: Dodgebull.

Knock, knock.

Who's there?

Waddle.

Waddle who?

Waddle we do when we get to the lake?

Lisa: Why did Mom buy marshmal-lows?

Leah: She said we needed s'more.

Q: Why did the skier want to go home?

A: He was snow-bored.

Q: How do you buy a map for your trip?

A: You pay the geogra-fee.

Q: What has eighteen wheels and running shoes?

A: A truck and fielder.

Q: Why was the baseball player thirsty?

A: He couldn't find his pitcher.

Q: What do you get when you cross a surfboard and a handkerchief?

A: A boogie board.

Q: Where do baseball players eat their dinner?

A: At home plate.

Trapeze artist #1: Do you like your job at the circus?

Trapeze artist #2: I'm getting into the swing of things.

Q: What do you get when you cross dynamite and a telephone?

A: A boomerang!

Q: What's an astronaut's favorite game?

A: Moon-opoly.

Mom: Do you think it will be a nice hotel?

Dad: I have reservations.

Q: How is Hawaii like your arms?

A: Hawaii has tourists, and your arms have two wrists.

Q: What happened when the river was naughty?

A: It got paddled.

Knock, knock.

Who's there?

Safari.

Safari who?

Safari like this funny joke book!

Q: What's the craziest animal in

   Africa?

A: A hyper-potamus!

Q: What's a frog's favorite game?

A: Croak-et.

Knock, knock.

   Who's there?

Atlas.

   Atlas who?

Atlas you're answering the door!

Q: Where do pigs like to relax?

A: In a ham-mock.

Q: Why did the horse need a suitcase?

A: It was a globe-trotter.

Q: Where does a peach take a nap?

A: In an apri-cot.

Tammy: Have you heard of the planet Saturn?

Timmy: It has a ring to it.

Lucy: How much is a pair of binoculars?

Lara: I'm looking into it.

Brayden: Have you seen bigfoot?

Hayden: Not yeti!

Jordan: How are your scuba diving lessons going?

Justin: Swimmingly!

Logan: I caught fifty trout with just one worm.

Megan: That sounds a little fishy!

Q: Why did the tuba player go to the nurse?

A: He needed a band-age.

Q: How does a pirate clean his ship?

A: With a treasure mop!

Q: What does a cowboy put on his salad?

A: Ranch dressing.

Q: Why did the gardener put on her dancing shoes?

A: She was going to the hoe-down.

Q: Why do your little brothers always pick on you?

A: It's their expert-tease.

Q: How did the pilot get to the doctor?

A: She flu.

Q: What do you get when you give a rabbit a sleeping bag?

A: A hoppy camper!

Q: Why did the kid's pants fall down in choir?

A: He was belting it out!

Q: When do you bring a hammer on a hike?

A: When you want to hit the trail.

Q: Why did the boy do his homework on a trampoline?

A: So he could get a jump on it.

Andy: There's a skunk in my tent!

Mandy: That stinks.

Q: Why did the diver need a psychiatrist?

A: He was going off the deep end.

Q: What do you get when you cross a tree and chocolate ice cream?

A: A pine cone!

Q: Where do geologists play ball?

A: At the basketball quartz!

Janey: Do you want to look for fossils

with me?

Jamie: I dig it!

Knock, knock.

Who's there?

Judah.

Judah who?

Judah thought we'd go on vacation by

now.

Q: What kind of poems do you read in the woods?

A: Hike-u.

Q: Why do sea turtles watch the news?

A: To stay up on current events.

Q: How do you keep from losing your telescope?

A: You keep your eye on it.

Knock, knock.

Who's there?

Cashew.

Cashew who?

I'll cashew later.

Knock, knock.

Who's there?

Howdy.

Howdy who?

Howdy come up with this crazy joke?

Knock, knock.

Who's there?

Sherwood.

Sherwood who?

Sherwood be nice to reach our camp-site by now.

Harry: My mom won't let me ride the Ferris wheel.

Henry: That's not fair!

Q: How does your grandma give the very best presents?

A: Because she's gifted.

Q: Why did the fish go to jail?

A: Because it was gill-ty.

Knock, knock.

Who's there?

Taylor.

Taylor who?

Taylor it's time to go to the movies.

Q: Why do football players get good grades?

A: They tackle their homework every night.

Q: **Why are forest rangers so honest and reliable?**

A: It's in their nature.

Q: **Why did the astronaut eat steak instead of salad?**

A: She wanted something meteor.

Q: **Does everybody drink soda?**

A: It's pop-ular!

Q: **Why are boxers never thirsty?**

A: They always beat you to the punch.

Q: How did the secret agent feel when he couldn't crack the code?

A: He was re-Morse-ful.

Jerry: My campsite is better than yours!

Larry: Don't be so pre-tent-ious.

Q: How does it feel to climb a mountain?

A: Ex-hill-arating!

Q: When is a rabbit's foot unlucky?

A: When you're the rabbit.

Q: Why did the astronaut forget his helmet?

A: He was spacey.

Q: Why did the grizzly join the choir?

A: It was a bear-itone.

Knock, knock.

Who's there?

Alto.

Alto who?

Alto the boat to the lake.

Q: How do you play hide-and-seek in the desert?

A: You wear camel-flage.

Q: Why don't we tell jokes about macaroni?

A: They're too cheesy.

Roger: Did you hit my car on purpose?

Roper: No, it was just a coinci-dents.

Q: What happens when your foot falls asleep?

A: It's coma-toes.

Rita: Can you tell me if you brushed your teeth this morning?

Lisa: No, it's confi-dental.

Q: What do you get when you cross a dog and a lobster?

A: A Doberman pincher.

Marney: What happens if bigfoot steps on your toe?

Millie: He'll Sasquatch it.

Knock, knock.

Who's there?

Italy.

Italy who?

Italy a shame if we don't play outside today.

Q: What do you eat underwater?

A: Sub sandwiches.

Q: Why did the kids want to play in the snow?

A: It was ent-icing.

Q: What kind of car does the sun like to drive?

A: An S-UV.

Q: Why did the skunks disappear?

A: They became ex-stinked.

Mandy: My dog brought me a stick all the way from South America.

Mindy: That sounds far-fetched.

Q: What do you call a stinky castle?

A: A fart-ress.

Q: How do you become a conductor?

A: Lots of training!

Q: Why was the astronaut crying?

A: He was a rocket-tear.

Q: What do you eat in a treehouse?

A: A club sandwich.

Q: Did you hear about the giant cow?

A: It's legen-dairy!

Sam: I forgot to pack my bug spray!

Cam: That bites.

Gary: Did you see the movie about the unicorn?

Mary: I'd never myth it!

Q: Where do wasps go on vacation?

A: To the bee-ch.

Q: What did one atom say to the other?

A: You matter.

Q: Why couldn't the skunk make a phone call?

A: It was out of odor.

Q: What did one clown say to the other?

A: You smell funny.

Q: Why did the captain buy a new ship?

A: It was on sail.

Q: What do beavers put on their salads?

A: Branch dressing.

- - - - - - - - - - - - - - - - - - - -

<u>Tongue Twisters:</u>

Mushy marshmallows.

Sort your sport shorts.

Lizards slither.

Slick sticks slip.

Seals steal shells.

Grandpa's cramped camper.

Felines feel fine.

Knock, knock.

Who's there?

Diesel.

Diesel who?

Diesel be the last knock-knock joke in this book!